0352.

BUS SCENE IN COLOUR:
PRESERVED BUSES

GAVIN BOOTH & PETER DURHAM

IAN ALLAN
Publishing

First published 1997

ISBN 0 7110 2537 1

© Peter Durham 1997

Published by Ian Allan Publishing

an imprint of Ian Allan Ltd, Terminal House, Station Approach, Shepperton, Surrey TW17 8AS.
Printed by Ian Allan Printing Ltd at its works at Coombelands in Runnymede, England.

Code: 9709/B3

Front cover:
Outwardly a typical municipal AEC Regent III with Roe bodywork, this 1951 9613A variant was new to Doncaster Corporation as No 122, with several experimental features. It lasted with Doncaster only until 1955 when it was sold to local independent, Blue Ensign. It was subsequently bought and restored by Tony Peart. *All photographs by Peter Durham*

Back cover:
Bristol chassis with ECW bodies loom large in the lists of preserved buses and coaches. This 1970 Bristol RELH6L has dual-purpose 49-seat ECW bodywork and was new as Bristol Omnibus No 2062, working from Bath, Wells, Gloucester and Stroud garages. Stroud can be seen in the valley behind the bus. It is now owned by the Stroud RE Group.

Title page:
This Regal III with distinctive Burlingham 33-seat coach body was new to Florence Motors of Morecambe in 1948, fleet No 23, but after two years passed to Cooper Bros, part of United Services of Pontefract. *Thanks to Anna Farrer and Stephan Torres*

Introduction

Now it can be told! When Peter Durham first submitted a selection of his photographs to *Classic Bus*, I rejected them. They were undoubtedly well taken, but they were preserved buses at rallies — something I have tried to avoid in the pages of the magazine.

Fortunately, Peter didn't give up. He doesn't, as those who have submitted their buses to the Durham treatment will readily testify. He sent a further selection, suggesting that I should think again. These were in the style we now recognise as Peter's own, and I was happy to eat my words. I started using at least one of his photos in each issue, and managed the odd photo-feature as well. Since then Peter's work has featured in *Classic Bus Yearbooks* and *Classic Bus* calendars, as well as a range of other magazines, and vehicle owners are queuing up to have their prize possessions photographed.

Peter's photos are mostly 645 medium format which ensures excellent reproduction, but before you rush out to buy Bronicas or Mamiyas it is worth pointing out that Peter also uses a Nikon F4S 35mm camera, and one of the photos in this book — I won't say which! — is taken on the smaller format. This should offer encouragement to the majority of enthusiasts who have armed themselves with hundreds of pounds worth of 35mm gear.

Watching Peter at work is an education — and an exercise in patience. He will travel from his Gloucestershire home to most parts of the UK, usually driven by the faithful Carol who can usually be found somewhere in attendance, laden down with camera equipment and vainly trying to change a film in the most adverse conditions. Peter is not content with the snatched photos that many of us rely on. He will search out a perfect setting and wait for the ideal weather conditions before his finger even hovers over the shutter release. He is a perfectionist, and this shows in the selection of his bus studies in this book.

Normally in a book like this it is important to achieve a good balance in the choice of photos — with a fair representation of vehicle types and operators. This hasn't been so easy with this book. Peter often photographs buses by invitation, and we found that there was a significant number of buses in southwest England, and, inevitably perhaps given the composition of the preserved bus 'fleet', a goodly quantity of AECs, Bristols and Leylands. The photos are arranged alphabetically, by manufacturer.

A great deal of time and effort goes into all of Peter's photographs. He is not, as many believe, a professional photographer, even though his pictures are of professional quality. He is involved in higher education and, like the rest of us, takes his photos when he can — at weekends and during holidays.

Bus Preservation

Looking at the 6,000-plus buses and coaches that are preserved in the UK today, it would be natural to assume that this fleet had been built up over the past 50 or 60 years. But in truth, bus preservation is a remarkably recent phenomenon.

As recently as 1961 the magazine *Buses Illustrated* was listing the 81 buses that represented the entire complement of preserved buses. By the end of the 1960s there were a handful of rallies taking place around the country; so few that enthusiasts could — and some did — attend every one. By the 1970s the momentum was really starting, and by the 1980s the movement had really taken off.

Many of the early buses were 'officially' preserved, by far-sighted operators like London Transport and organisations like the British Transport Commission which recognised the need to preserve important parts of our transport heritage. For individuals the prospect of saving a bus often seemed daunting, and many pioneering preservation efforts fell through simply because of lack of confidence.

In that 1961 list there were 43 privately preserved buses, many under the care of the Vintage Passenger Vehicle Society, which was formed by pioneers like Prince Marshall, Ken Blacker and Michael Dryhurst who first got together in 1956 to try their hand at preservation and restoration. Others were from the collection of Colin Shears, another of the small band of pioneering preservationists.

As the movement grew so did the expertise of the owners. People who had no first-hand experience found themselves becoming expert engineers, electricians, coachbuilders and painters, and as preservationists met others with a similar interest, collections were formed with vehicles sharing common accommodation, and owners sharing their experiences.

The rally calendar grew, with long-standing events like the Trans-Pennine Run and the London-Brighton Run joined by rallies in every part of the country. Some were solely bus events; at others, buses shared the spotlight with cars, commercials, steam wagons, tractors and steam locomotives.

Then the running day came along: an opportunity to ride on older buses, often on their original routes, and these have sprung up all over Britain.

Today it is not difficult to see and enjoy older buses and coaches. From Easter through to October there is a bewildering choice of events. Each April *Buses* magazine publishes its rally calendar; the 1997 edition listed 147 events. There are also the static collections: some are vehicle stores with limited public access; others are run as museums with voluntary help; others, most notably the London Transport Museum, are commercial ventures.

Bus preservation has come a long way in little more than 30 years, and Peter Durham's fine photographs show a splendid selection of the buses and coaches that have been restored by loving owners and represent many, many hours of blood, sweat and tears, as well as considerable amounts of money. There are many more buses in course of restoration, and hundreds that are simply set aside safely, to be worked on at some time in the future.

If you are interested in getting involved in bus preservation, speak to any of the owners at rallies, running days or museums; if they can't make use of you, they will probably suggest someone who can. And you never know — one day you might be standing watching Peter Durham photograph your pride and joy.

A list of museums is given on page 5. For full details of opening times etc, see the Museum Guide published each April in *Buses* magazine. Give these museums your support; in them you will see some of the buses and coaches featured in this book, as well as many more splendid reminders of the great days of the British bus — some immaculately restored, others being worked on, and others still in their 'as-rescued' state.

Gavin Booth
Edinburgh
April 1997

Right:
The Associated Equipment Company (AEC) had its roots in the London General Omnibus Company, but since 1912 had been a separate commercial business. Although AEC was still the principal supplier of bus chassis to London Transport, it built up a substantial business building trucks and buses for customers in the UK and overseas before it merged with Leyland in 1962. The last AEC bus chassis were built in 1979.

The Regal was AEC's principal front-engined single-deck bus and coach model from 1929 until the 1950s. The original models had petrol engines and many of the last home market models had the sophisticated combination of AEC's 9.6-litre engine and preselective transmission.

The AEC Regal II was a lighter-weight model introduced in 1935. Many of the surviving chassis of all types from the late 1930s were rebodied in the postwar period to prolong their lives, and this 1937 Trent example was rebodied in 1950 with this Willowbrook 35-seat coach body. No 714 is now part of the Birmingham & Midland Museum of Transport (BaMMOT) collection at Wythall.

Acknowledgements

Peter and I are indebted to the vehicle owners and drivers who arrange to make their buses and coaches available, drive them to suitable spots and position them to suit Peter's critical eye. We are happy to acknowledge their help as indicated in the 'credits' to individual illustrations.

Below:
The AEC Regal I was introduced in 1946 with the 7.7-litre engine and crash gearbox. This 1947 example, with Weymann 35-seat bus body, was new to the Devon General company, a faithful AEC customer for many years, and is seen in a delightful Devon lane *en route* to Exeter. It was withdrawn after only 10 years, working mainly from the Newton Abbot garage. Over a 25-year period it was restored to its original condition.

Museums mentioned in this book

Birmingham & Midland Museum of Transport (BaMMOT), Chapel Lane, Wythall B47 6JX (tel: 01564 826471)

Black Country Living Museum, Tipton Road, Dudley, West Midlands (tel: 0121 557 9643)

Cobham Bus Museum (London Bus Preservation Trust), Redhill Road, Cobham, Surrey KT11 1EF (tel: 01932 868665)

East Anglia Transport Museum, Chapel Road, Carlton Colville, Lowestoft, Suffolk (tel: 01502 518459)

Lincolnshire Vintage Vehicle Society, Whisby Road, Lincoln (tel: 01522 689497)

Manchester Museum of Transport, Boyle Street, Cheetham, Manchester (tel: 0161 205 2122)

National Tramway Museum, Crich, Matlock, Derbyshire DE4 5DP (tel: 01773 852326)

Oxford Bus Museum, Old Station Yard, Long Hanborough (tel: 01865 400002)

Sandtoft Transport Centre, Belton Road, Sandtoft, nr Doncaster DN8 5SX (tel: 01724 711391)

Scottish Vintage Bus Museum, Lathalmond, Fife (tel: 01383 720241)

Other museums

Amberley Museum, Arundel, West Sussex

Aston Manor Road Transport Museum, Witton Lane, Birmingham

Bournemouth Transport Museum, Mallard Road depot, Bournemouth

British Commercial Vehicle Museum, Leyland, Lancashire

Castle Point Transport Museum, Canvey Island, Essex

City of Portsmouth Preserved Transport Depot, Old Portsmouth

Dewsbury Bus Museum, Dewsbury, West Yorkshire

Dover Transport Museum, Whitfield, Dover

Glasgow Museum of Transport, Kelvin Hall, Glasgow

Ipswich Transport Museum, Ipswich

Keighley Bus Museum, Denholme, Keighley, West Yorkshire

London Transport Museum, Covent Garden, London

Meltham Mills Bus Museum, Huddersfield

The North of England Open Air Museum, Beamish, Co Durham

Nottingham Heritage Centre, Ruddington, Nottinghamshire

Rushden Historical Transport Society, Old Rushden railway station, Northamptonshire

Seaton Tramway, Seaton, Devon

Sheffield Bus Museum, Tinsley, Sheffield

Summerlea Heritage Park, Coatbridge, North Lanarkshire

Tameside Transport Collection, Mossley, Manchester

Transperience, Bradford

Transport Museum Society of Ireland, Howth, Co Dublin

Ulster Folk & Transport Museum, Cultra, Co Down

Wirral Transport Museum, Birkenhead, Merseyside

Above:
How many preserved buses start in this condition? There are many far worse than this that are eventually rebuilt to appear in as-built condition — some perhaps better than as-built condition, it must be said. This 1956 Nottingham Corporation AEC Regent V, No 229, with 61-seat Park Royal bodywork was photographed at the Oxford Bus Museum in 1995, awaiting attention. Many months, often years, of blood, sweat and tears go into the restoration of the buses you see in this book, and it is worthwhile remembering where it can often start.

Left:
Another 1948 Regal III, this time with Windover 32-seat coach bodywork of the style modelled by the diecast manufacturer Exclusive First Editions. New to Trent, it is now owned by John Burton of Alfreton, and is seen at the nearby National Tramway Museum at Crich.

Above:
Fully-fronted bodies were popular for later front-engined coaches, and this AEC Regal III of 1950 has full-fronted Harrington coachwork. Its only commercial operator was Bevan Bros (Soudley Coaches), and it is seen at Selsley, overlooking the Stroud Valley, re-creating the evening Cotswold Mystery Tour. *Thanks to Nick Helliker*

Left:
A more unusual body style on AEC Regal III chassis was the Hull-built Barnaby. This 35-seat coach, in the distinguished colours of York Pullman, was new in 1954 as fleet No 66, and was at one time team coach for the York City football club and the York rugby league team. It lasted with the company until 1971, when it passed into preservation.
Thanks to Stephan Torres and Jeff Colledge

Above:
The front-engined Regal was largely replaced by the underfloor-engined Regal IV, first introduced in 1949. This used a horizontal version of the 9.6-litre engine in a substantial chassis, and London Transport chose this model as its standard postwar single-decker. Some 700 RF-class Regal IVs joined LT between 1951 and 1953, the great majority with 7ft 6in-wide Metro-Cammell bodywork. No RF534 was new in 1952 as a 39-seat Central Area bus, and ended its service days at Kingston garage, being one of the few to carry white relief lining.
Thanks to Mike Nash of the London Bus Preservation Group, at whose Cobham premises No RF534 was photographed

Left:
Representing the green-painted London Transport RFs, No RF672, a 41-seat bus, was new in October 1953 to East Grinstead garage in the Country Area, and was retired from Staines garage in January 1972.
Thanks to Paul Morris and David Jones

Left:

The weight of early underfloor-engined models like the AEC Regal IV led manufacturers to develop lighter-weight chassis to satisfy demands for more fuel-efficient buses and coaches. The Reliance was AEC's version, a chassis that remained in production from 1953 to 1979. The Reliance was a popular choice for bus and coach work; this 1956 example has Burlingham 44-seat bus body and was new to the well-known independent, Safeguard of Guildford, passing in 1963 to Safeway Services of South Petherton, Somerset, who ran it until 1982. It is restored in Safeway colours. *Thanks to Hugh Jones*

Above:

Roe was better known for its bus bodies, but in the 1950s it offered the Dalesman coach body. New to West Riding in 1957 as No 803, this Reliance MU3RV has 41-seat centre-entrance Roe bodywork. It was withdrawn in 1966. It was bought for restoration in 1992 by David Crowther and is now owned by Classic Coaches of High Wycombe and has been restored to psv status as an operating coach.

Left:
Devon General's coach fleet, Grey Cars, bought this Reliance with 7ft 6in-wide Willowbrook 41-seat coach body in 1959 for touring work on Dartmoor, where the narrower width was useful. No 890 was transferred to Greenslades and Royal Blue before being finally retired by Western National in 1980.
Thanks to Martin Gibbons

Right:
This style of Alexander body was built from 1957 to 1962, mainly for Scottish Bus Group fleets. New to the giant Alexander fleet in 1960, this Reliance 2MU3RV with 41-seat coach body passed to the newly-formed Alexander Northern company the following year. Fleet No NAC147 was based at Elgin depot.
Thanks to Gavin F. Booth and Lawrence Macduff of the West of Scotland Bus Group

Above:
City of Oxford was a confirmed AEC user, and this is a 1960 AEC Reliance
2MU3RV with Park Royal 44-seat bodywork, No 756. It was withdrawn in 1973,
passing to Chukie Chickens as a staff bus, but is now back in original livery and based
at the Oxford Bus Museum. *Thanks to Neil Tidbury*

Right:
Plaxton coach bodies became more popular in the 1960s and 1970s, and the Scarborough company eventually overtook the former market leader, Duple. This 1961 AEC Reliance 2MU3RV has a 41-seat Plaxton Embassy coach body with centre entrance, a layout favoured by some operators after front entrances became widely accepted. It was new to the large Wakefield-based independent operator, West Riding, No 917, and passed to Imperial Coachways of Windsor in 1968, who retained it for a further 17 years. *Thanks to C. J. Birch*

Below:
David MacBrayne was one of the best-loved bus and coach operators, until it was absorbed into the fleets of Scottish Bus Group companies in 1970-2. Fortunately a number of MacBrayne vehicles are preserved, including these two AEC Reliances. On the left is a 1961 2MU3RA example with Duple Donington 41-seat coach bodywork, new to the Oban garage as No 63. Alongside is 1967 2U3RA Reliance No 150 with 49-seat Willowbrook coach body. Both vehicles passed to Highland Omnibuses in 1970.
Thanks to Derek Hunter, Graham Murray and Lawrence Macduff

Left:
This 1962 Reliance 2MU3RA has Duple Britannia 43-seat coach bodywork, and was new to Don's of Southsea, passing quite quickly to Chiltern Queens of Woodcote It is now stored at the Oxford Bus Museum. *Thanks to John Bayliss*

Above:
The big-windowed Panorama coach body helped to put Plaxton firmly on the map as Britain's leading coachbuilder. This 1968 AEC Reliance has 41-seat Panorama I bodywork and was new to Neath & Cardiff Luxury Coaches, best remembered for its Swansea-Cardiff express service. A BET group company for many years, N&C passed into the control of the South Wales company in 1971. *Thanks to Jeffrey Phillips*

Above:
The double-deck equivalent of AEC's Regal model was the Regent, built from 1929 to 1968. Morecambe & Heysham Corporation No 20 was new in 1948, a Regent III 6811A model with 7.7-litre engine and crash gearbox. It carries 59-seat highbridge Park Royal bodywork and was operated by its original owner, and its post-reorganisation successor, Lancaster City Transport, until 1978.

Right:
Another Park Royal-bodied AEC Regent III, Halifax Joint Omnibus Committee No 277, was new in 1950 and is now used on bus services in the Halifax area. In 1996 Tony Blackman and his wife Gloria set up the Halifax Joint Committee to operate the Calderdale Heritage Trail Bus between Halifax and Hebden Bridge.
Thanks to Tony Blackman

Above:
Carrying a later style of Park Royal bodywork on AEC Regent III chassis, Nottingham City Transport No 161 was new in 1953, being retired in 1967 when it passed to Grimsby-Cleethorpes Transport for the sum of £310. Restoration to its original livery was completed by Nottingham Heritage Centre during 1995.
Thanks to Steve Powell

Right:
A rare body style on AEC Regent III, the rounded four-bay design built by Alexander in the early 1950s. Dundee Corporation No 137 had a 58-seat body and ran in Dundee from 1953 until 1975. It is now preserved at the Scottish Vintage Bus Museum in Fife.

Left:
Although AEC offered a full-width front on the AEC Regent V when it was introduced in 1954, some operators specified the traditional AEC radiator. This is City of Oxford No H956, a 1957 Regent V with stylish Park Royal 61-seat highbridge bodywork. Withdrawn in 1970, it is now owned by Michael Freeman and based at the Oxford Bus Museum.
Thanks to Neil Tidbury

Below:
Barton Transport was one of the most individual and enterprising bus and coach companies in Britain, and the name survives today as part of the Trent empire. The Barton family still owns No 851, a 1960 AEC Regent V with Northern Counties 70-seat forward-entrance bodywork, featuring a full-width front and curved front screens, and the bus is on permanent loan to the Nottingham Heritage Centre. It was withdrawn in 1973 and became a driver trainer before joining the Barton cherished fleet; it is seen as preserved on its old Ruddington-Nottingham route.
Thanks to Phil Sharpe, Simon Bramley and Steve Powell

Left:
One of the most famous bus types of all time, the London Transport Routemaster, built by AEC and Park Royal between 1958 and 1968, although the prototype had appeared in 1954. Geoff Rixon's RM254 is one of the best-known preserved examples.
Thanks to Geoff Rixon

Left:
Most Regent Vs had 'new-look' fronts incorporating an attractive AEC grille, like No 63, this 1964 Ipswich Corporation example with 65-seat Massey bodywork, now part of the Ipswich Transport Museum collection. *Thanks to Mark Smith*

Above:
AEC introduced the lowheight Bridgemaster model in 1956, but this did not prove to be one of its most successful models. Only 179 were built. This 1963 Bridgemaster for East Yorkshire has a specially-tapered upper deck profile to allow it to pass through the Beverley Bar. *Thanks to Roger Beckett*

Right:
Albion built cars and commercial vehicle chassis at Scotstoun, Glasgow, from 1899 and although the company was taken over by Leyland in 1951, it continued to develop and build bus and truck models until the 1980s. This fine normal control Victor model with 20-seat sunroof body by Abbott of Farnham was new in 1935 to the famous Winchester independent, King Alfred Motor Services. *Thanks to Dave Hurley*

Left:
Atkinson, best known for truck models, dabbled in the bus market between 1950 and 1963. It built this unique PD746 double-decker in 1954 for the Stalybridge, Hyde, Mossley & Dukinfield Transport & Electricity Board, operating services in the east of the Manchester conurbation. Centre-entrance 59-seat Northern Counties bodywork is fitted to No 70. It is now part of the Manchester Museum of Transport collection.
Thanks to Dennis Talbot and Mark Prescott

Above:
The largest of the English company operators, Birmingham & Midland Motor Omnibus Company, better known by its Midland Red fleetname, built buses and coaches, principally for its own use, from 1924. Known for its technical advances, BMMO-built models dominated the Midland Red fleet until the last examples appeared in 1970. This is an S15 model, an integrally-built dual-purpose vehicle. No 5056 was new to Hereford garage in 1962, often working the Hereford-Leicester service. It was withdrawn in 1972 and passed through various owners before being acquired for preservation. *Thanks to Roy Wagstaff*

Above:
This BMMO S17 model with Willowbrook 52-seat bus body, No 5479, entered service at the Markfield garage in Leicestershire in 1964 and operated from various garages in the county. It was restored by the Worcester Bus Preservation Society.
Thanks to Rupert Chambers and Chris Martin

Right:
Vauxhall Motors introduced its Bedford range of commercial vehicles in 1931 and these quickly became very popular. The best-loved Bedford model is probably the semi-normal control OB, typically with Duple Vista coach bodywork. This OB was new to SMT in 1947 as No C167 with an SMT Vista body, but was rebuilt and rebodied after only six years, receiving this full-fronted Burlingham Baby Seagull 24-seat body for coach tours to the Scottish Highlands and Islands.
Thanks to Tom Forsyth

Left:
A more typical Bedford OB is this 1951 example with Duple Vista 29-seat body. It was new to Wye Valley Coaches of Hereford, and is now owned by another operator, Boultons of Shropshire, which uses it regularly for private hire work.

Above:
In 1950 Bedford replaced the OB with the forward control SB model, which remained on the lists until the end of Bedford bus production in 1987. Duple coach bodywork continued to be a popular choice. This 1962 SB3 has a Duple Super Vega body and was new to Crimson Tours of St Ives, Cornwall; it passed to Birds of Hunstanton in 1965. *Thanks to Len Wright and Malcolm Robinson*

Above:

The Bristol Tramways & Carriage Company started building bus chassis for its own operations in 1908 and from 1920 these were available for other operators. By the end of the 1930s, Bristol chassis were becoming a standard purchase for other fleets in the Tilling group, often carrying bodywork by fellow Tilling company Eastern Coach Works of Lowestoft. After World War 2, Bristol and ECW passed into state control, following the nationalisation of the mainline railway companies who held a substantial stake in Tilling. Between 1948 and 1965 Bristol chassis and ECW bodies were available only to state-owned companies, but following a share exchange with Leyland, Bristol and ECW products returned to the open market, until the factories were closed by Leyland in the 1980s. Bristol chassis designations included a reference to engine type: 4A was the four-cylinder Albion engine; 5G the Gardner 5LW; 6G the Gardner 6LW or 6LX; 6L the Leyland O.600 or O.680.

The L was Bristol's single-deck model from 1937, and it was reintroduced after World War 2. No 262 was new to Southern National in 1938 as an L5G model, with Beadle bodywork; it was war-damaged in Plymouth, receiving a utility Mumford body. In 1955 it was lengthened to become an LL5G at Bideford, receiving a new ECW 39-seat rear-entrance bus body.

Thanks to Dave Johnson and the Cotswold

Above:
At first glance an ECW body, this 1939 Western National Bristol L5G carries a 1950 Beadle 35-seat rear-entrance bus body. New to Plymouth garage, No 333 ended its Western National days as a messroom at Launceston in 1961. It is now owned by the Gloucester-based 333 Bus Preservation Group. *Thanks to Tim Riley*

Left:
Another L5G rebody is North Western No 270, a 1946 example which had originally carried a Brush body, but received this Willowbrook 38-seat rear-entrance bus body in 1953.

Right:
Converted in 1960 to forward-entrance layout for driver-only operation, United Automobile Services No BG413 is an L5G new in 1949. It has been restored by Aycliffe & District Bus Preservation Society.
Thanks to Roy Lambeth

Left:
Crosville No SLG147 was an L5G new in 1949 as KG147, but was renumbered in 1958. It entered service at Llandudno Junction and when it was withdrawn from service it passed to Cheshire Constabulary as a mobile exhibition vehicle.
Thanks to Ray Jones and Llewelyn Williams

Above:
Bristol's double-deck equivalent to the L was the K, built between 1937 and 1957. This 1940 K5G, No C3336, was one of 200 built to replace the Bristol trams. The highbridge body was built by the Brislington Body Works (BBW), Bristol's bodybuilding department. It was withdrawn in 1950, being acquired by the Bristol Vintage Bus Group in 1973 and completely restored by them to the livery used by the Bristol company until the war.
Thanks to the Bristol Vintage Bus Group and Lionel Tancock

Right:
In the more familiar Tilling green livery of Bristol Omnibus Company, a late-model (1955) KSW6B with 60-seat highbridge ECW body, No C8322. First registered in January 1956, it was withdrawn in 1972 and preserved.
Thanks to Adrian Hunt and Bob Archer

Left:
The underfloor-engined semi-integral Bristol LS became the standard Tilling Group single-deck model when it was introduced in 1952, and all but a handful carried ECW bus or coach bodies. Eastern National No 1237, new in 1955, was an LS5G, with 45-seat ECW bus body. It was retired from Brentwood garage in 1976.
Thanks to C. R. Salmon and Peter Blake

Above:
The Bristol LS was replaced in 1957 by the MW, a separate chassis. Again, all but a handful of MWs received ECW bodies. This West Yorkshire Road Car example, No EUG71, an MW5G model, has 41-seat dual-purpose ECW bodywork and was new to Bradford depot in 1958. It was sold on to Lincolnshire Road Car in 1972.
Thanks to Neil Halliday and Ian Hunter

Above:
Eastern National No 350 is a 1961 Bristol MW5G with the restrained yet stylish ECW
coach body of the time, with seats for 35 passengers. It was based at Braintree garage
and used on British and Continental tours. In 1973 it was sold to a dealer and then
acquired by King's School, Chester; it was later rescued for preservation. It was
photographed in rural Dorset *en route* for Bournemouth. *Thanks to John Hallett*

Left:
A 1963 Bristol MW5G with ECW dual-purpose 43-seat body from the Bristol Omnibus fleet. It is seen at the National Tramway Museum at Crich, Derbyshire, and is regular transport for the 1st Stretford Scout Group.
Thanks to Keith Chadbourne

Above:
In the Bristol Greyhound livery used by Bristol Omnibus for its coach fleet between 1961 and 1973, 1965 MW6G No 2572 with ECW 39-seat coach body was used on Associated Motorways services to South Coast resorts until 1971 when it was relegated to bus duties. *Thanks to the late Ted Amos*

Above:
Another MW6G in Bristol Greyhound livery, No 2150 carries the later style of ECW coach body on this chassis, first introduced in 1962. New in 1966, this 39-seat coach was withdrawn during the 1973/4 season. *Thanks to Bryan Sharpe*

Right:
Bristol and ECW catered for the limited demand for smaller and lighter buses for rural work with a series of single-deck models. The SU had an underfloor-mounted Albion engine, and this SUL4A with 33-seat ECW body was new in 1962 to Western National and passed via Guernseybus to Tillingbourne Bus Company for further service. *Thanks to John Tyekiff*

Right:
Bristol revolutionised single-deck design with the introduction of the rear-engined RE model in 1962, the first, and to many the best, of the rear-engined chassis introduced in the 1960s. Brighton Hove & District No 206, an RESL6G model with two-door ECW 35-seat body, was new in 1968 and passed into the Southdown fleet when BH&D was placed under Southdown control in 1969. Withdrawn in 1981, it saw further service with independent operators before being purchased for restoration. *Thanks to Adrian Henson*

Left:
After Bristol and ECW products came back on to the open market in 1965, many operators chose to buy them. Colchester Corporation built up a fleet of 15 ECW-bodied Bristol RELL6Ls, and No 24 of 1972 was bought for preservation after service with G&G Coaches, Leamington Spa. *Thanks to Guy Stanbury*

Right:
United Auto ran the prototype Bristol RE and went on to build up a sizeable fleet. No 6080 was a 1973 RELH6G with ECW dual-purpose 49-seat body which was based at Darlington, Ripon and Bishop Auckland before retirement in 1988. It is seen re-creating a scene on the 22A Stockton-Darlington route.
Thanks to Bryan Sharpe

Left:
Several operators specified two-door VRTs, including City of Oxford, whose No 476, a 1977 VRTSL6G with 70-seat ECW body, demonstrates the later style of front with BET-style windscreen. It carries traditional City of Oxford livery, to mark the centenary of the company in 1981.
Thanks to Graham Wareham and the Oxford Bus Museum

Right:
In 1946 AEC and Leyland combined their trolleybus manufacturing interests as British United Traction (BUT). This AEC-built BUT 9611T model with Weymann 56-seat bodywork was new to Brighton Corporation in 1947, entering service as No 52 in 1951 and passing to Maidstone Corporation in 1959, again as No 52. It is seen under the wires at the East Anglia Transport Museum at Carlton Colville, near Lowestoft.

Left:
Chevrolet was one of a number of American builders who tried to break into the UK market with smaller chassis. This 1929 LQ model with 13-seat Spicer body in the livery of White Heather Lakeland Tours re-creates one of its early Lake District tours from Morecambe, which continued until the early 1950s. These offered a 134-mile tour for 12s 6d (62½p). It is now housed at the Lincolnshire Road Transport Museum in Lincoln. *Thanks to Bob Brewer*

Above:
Commer Cars Ltd competed with Bedford for the lighter-weight coach market in the 1950s, but never achieved Bedford's market penetration. This Commer Avenger IV, fitted with the unusual two-stroke TS3 engine, carries Plaxton Embassy 41-seat coach bodywork still in the original 1962 paint of its first owner, Wrights of Wrexham — although it is lettered for its second owner, John G. Jones of Penybont. It was photographed in May evening sunshine in the Marches of England to the west of Bishop's Castle. *Thanks to Russell Price*

Right:
Crossley built bus and coach chassis at Manchester and Stockport between 1928 and 1953, though from 1948 the company was part of Associated Commercial Vehicles (ACV), in company with AEC and Maudslay. The main postwar single-deck model was the SD42, and this 1948 SD42/7 with Plaxton 33-seat coach body was owned by Albert Davies Transport, and a daily visitor to Our Lady of Zion Convent at Acton Burnell Hall, Shropshire, where its 1950 duties were re-created.
Thanks to Tony Morris of Concorde College and Andrew Davies

Above:
Daimler was one of the best-known names in the British motor industry, building buses between 1908 and 1980 when, under Leyland ownership since 1968, production of the Fleetline was moved from Daimler's traditional home in Coventry to Leyland, Lancashire. The postwar CV single-deck model was offered with AEC 7.7-litre, Daimler CD6, or Gardner 5LW or 6LW engines, and this 1948 CVD6 (Daimler engine) has a Willowbrook 35-seat bus body. It was new to the famous independent operator, Venture Transport of Consett, fleet No 156.
Thanks to Harry Bunney

Right:
The Daimler CV range of double-deck chassis was built from 1946 until 1968 and was a popular choice among municipal operators, of which there were nearly 100 until the late 1960s. Aberdeen Corporation bought this CVG6 with 66-seat Alexander body in 1965, No 325.

SCATTERBURN 24

325

CRG 325C

53

Right:
Although Dennis buses are very familiar today, during the 1950s they tended to be bought by a dwindling band of faithful customers. Most notable among these was the 'local' operator, Aldershot & District, which continued to buy Dennis chassis until 1965. Two Aldershot & District examples of the Lance double-deck chassis are seen here, both with East Lancs bodywork. Nearer the camera is No 220, a 1954 Lance K4 model with the Dennis version of the 'new-look' front and 56-seat lowbridge bodywork; this bus spent its life at Aldershot garage before withdrawal in 1965. Behind is No 145, a 1950 Lance K3 with a 51-seat lowbridge body, new to Hindhead garage and withdrawn in 1962. *Thanks to Tim Stubbs*

Above:
Also new in 1965, a Daimler Fleetline CRG6LX with Alexander D-type lowheight bodywork, No 174 in the North Western Road Car fleet, but carrying Selnec Cheshire vinyls, reflecting the situation following the split of the North Western company among various local operators. The Fleetline, introduced in 1960 and built until 1980, was Daimler's answer to the rear-engined Leyland Atlantean chassis.
Thanks to the Manchester Museum of Transport

Right:
Walsall Corporation, with R. Edgley Cox as General Manager, was famous for its innovative and unusual buses and trolleybuses. No 116 was one of over 100 short-length Daimler Fleetlines with Northern Counties dual-door bodies built to Walsall's specification. It is seen after restoration near Pleck Park, Walsall.
Thanks to Dave Taylor of the Birmingham & Midland Museum of Transport (BaMMOT)

Left:
Although it had built commercial chassis since 1914, it was the choice of Guy as one of the suppliers of utility double-deck chassis during World War 2 that propelled the company into the big league. The Arab model continued to be built after the war, and was also built as a single-deck chassis; this 1951 Arab III with 35-seat Roe coach body was new to the large independent, Lancashire United Transport, as No 440. Fitted with a Gardner 6LW engine, it later passed to Burmah Oil as a staff bus.
Thanks to Stephan Torres

Above:
Guy developed a special normal control chassis, designated NLLVP, for London Transport when it needed small buses to replace its Leyland Cubs on Country Area services. Perkins P6 engines were fitted and ECW built special 26-seat bodies. This 1953 example was new as London Transport GS2, and passed to Southern Motorways of Emsworth, Hampshire, in 1963, receiving the company's striking red/maroon/cream livery. *Thanks to Alan Bromley*

Above:
This Arab III with Guy-built 56-seat body was new in 1948; it was exhibited at the first postwar Commercial Motor Show that year before delivery to Lincoln Corporation as No 23. When new it had a Meadows 6DC630 engine, but in later life it received, unusually, a Leyland engine, and by the early 1960s had been fitted with a locally-built experimental Ruston & Hornsby air-cooled engine, noted for its noise and lively performance — hence the non-standard 'radiator'. It was withdrawn in 1967 and presented by Ruston & Hornsby to the Lincolnshire Vintage Vehicle Society. *Thanks to Steve Milner of the Lincolnshire Road Transport Museum*

Right:
In the early 1950s Birmingham City Transport built up a massive fleet of over 800 similar-looking standard double-deckers, based on Crossley, Daimler and Guy chassis. All featured what became known as the Birmingham 'new-look' front, and the bodies were fitted out to Birmingham's traditional high standards. No 2533 is a Guy Arab IV of 1950 with 54-seat Metro-Cammell bodywork, which lasted in service well into the West Midlands PTE era, being retired in October 1977 after 27 years' service. It is now preserved by the Acocks Green Preservation Group at the BaMMOT museum at Wythall. *Thanks to Fred Withers*

Above:
The standard wartime trolleybus model was the W4, built by Sunbeam in Wolverhampton, though a good proportion wore the Karrier badge of a sister company in the Rootes group. This Karrier W4 was new in 1946 to Bradford Corporation and in 1959 received a new East Lancs 66-seat forward-entrance body. Bradford, one of the first trolleybus operators in Britain in 1911, was also the last, in 1972. No 735 is seen at the Black Country Museum at Dudley.

Right:
Leyland grew from humble beginnings in 1896 to dominate the UK motor industry until the break-up of the company led to the sale of the bus interests to Volvo in 1988. When Leyland introduced its Titan double-deck model in 1927 it also launched a single-deck equivalent, the Tiger — a model which remained on the lists for 40 years, latterly as an export model. The massive Alexander company was a regular Tiger customer, buying over 200 in the postwar years. No PA44 was new in 1947, a Tiger PS1 with Alexander 35-seat dual-purpose body which spent most of its life at Buckie depot, in northeast Scotland. When the Alexander company was split into three in 1961 this bus became No NPA44 and received the yellow/cream livery of the new Alexander (Northern) company. *Thanks to Nigel Ainsworth*

Above:
Another 1947-built Leyland Tiger PS1 is this Jersey Motor Transport example with Leeds-built Wilks & Meade 35-seat bodywork. It was purchased in 1982 by the bus and coach operators, Davies Bros of Pencader. *Thanks to G. Evans*

Right:
Originally built for the Midland General company but diverted to Crosville, this 1950 Leyland Tiger PS1/1 has Metro-Cammell 35-seat bus bodywork. No ETE944 was based at Llandudno Junction and was withdrawn in 1964.
Thanks to Cliff Marsh and Phil Pixton

Above:
Leyland's initial underfloor-engined models, the Olympic and Royal Tiger, were big-engined heavyweight vehicles, but pressure from operators produced a new breed of lightweight chassis in the early 1950s, and Leyland's contribution was the Tiger Cub. This 1955 example has Harrington 41-seat coachwork and was new to the famous independent operator, Silver Star of Porton Down. It spent much of its life on express services to Edinburgh, Manchester and Swansea. It later passed, with the Silver Star business, to Western National, appearing in Royal Blue livery.
Thanks to Jack Parsons

Right:
A 1957 Tiger Cub with a Burlingham Seagull 41-seat coach body was new to Whittle of Highley. It is seen here at Highley station yard on the Severn Valley Railway alongside the preserved Ivatt 2-6-0 No 46443.
Thanks to SVR general manager Alun Rees, signalman Peter Gardener, driver John Price, fireman Jason Holders and coach owners Bernard and Sandra Rogers

Left:
A 1960 Tiger Cub PSUC1/2 with 41-seat dual-purpose Alexander body, new as PD177 in the Alexander fleet at Kelty, and passing on the 1961 split-up to the new Alexander (Fife) company until it was withdrawn in 1975. It is restored in its original Alexander cream/blue by the West of Scotland Bus Group.

Right:
Western Welsh built up a substantial fleet of Tiger Cubs. This late example, new in 1966, is a PSUC1/1 with 43-seat Park Royal body. New to Crosskeys garage, No 1370 was withdrawn in 1979, passing to the National Coal Board as a crew bus and was sold for scrap after the miners' strike, in 1986.
Thanks to Lee Jones

Right:
This Doncaster Corporation Tiger Cub was new in 1963 with a 45-seat Roe bus body. No 33 carries the livery style adopted in the undertaking's last years, before it was absorbed into South Yorkshire PTE. It is preserved by the Doncaster Omnibus and Light Railway Society at Sandtoft.

Left:
Mike Sutcliffe's amazing restorations of very early motorbuses have won him widespread praise and not a few awards. His 1996 offering was this 1908 Leyland X2 type, new to the London Central Motor Omnibus Company with bodywork by United Electric Car Co of Preston. LN 7270 is seen on Brighton's Madeira Drive after participating in the 1996 HCVS London-Brighton run, when it was outright *Concours d'Élégance* winner.

Above:
One of Leyland's most significant models was the Titan TD1, the first really modern double-decker, introduced in 1927. This introduced the lowbridge seating layout with its offside sunken gangway upstairs, a layout that lasted for the next 40 years, although by that time it had been rendered largely redundant by lower-built chassis. This 51-seat Leyland-bodied TD1 was new in 1928 to Glasgow Corporation, No 111, and afterwards spent many years as a static caravan in Kent. It has been restored to its original condition, as part of the Scottish Vintage Bus Museum collection at Lathalmond, Fife. *Thanks to Jasper Pettie and Dave Hoare*

Left:
Although AEC won the bulk of London Transport's double-deck orders, Leyland did pick up some useful business in the early postwar period supplying members of the growing RT family. These included 500 RTW types, built to the recently-sanctioned 8ft width. These were Londonised Leyland Titan PD2/3s with Leyland 56-seat bodies. No RTW29 was new in 1949 to Tottenham garage and operated from 11 central garages until withdrawn in 1969. *Thanks to Roy Adams*

Above:
The Titan continued to be Leyland's standard double-deck model after the war and was a popular choice with many fleets in the UK and overseas. Manchester Corporation bought this PD2/3 model, No 3245, in 1951, fitted with semi-streamlined Metro-Cammell 58-seat bodywork.
Thanks to Dennis Talbot and Mark Prescott of the Manchester Museum of Transport

Left:
Leyland built bodywork for its own chassis from its earliest days right through to 1954, and this Titan PD2/12 with Leyland Farington-style highbridge 58-seat bodywork was the last body built until Leyland restarted assembling bodies in the 1970s. This bus, now part of the BaMMOT collection, was new to Trent as No 1256. *Thanks to Paul Gray, Bob Lewis and Fred Withers*

Above:
Bolton Corporation was one of the many municipal fleets in the Greater Manchester area, all with their own idiosyncrasies when choosing new vehicles. Bolton No 77 is a 1956 Leyland Titan PD2/13 with exposed radiator and a Metro-Cammell Orion 62-seat body.
Thanks to Paul Williams and Mark Prescott of the Manchester Museum of Transport

Right:
The Leyland Titan PD3 range was introduced in 1956 following the relaxation of double-deck length regulations to allow 30ft-long buses. Many operators turned to forward-entrance bodies at this time, like this Yorkshire Woollen PD3A/1 with Metro-Cammell Orion 70-seat body, new in 1962 as No 893. It carries the later St Helens style of full-width front. It was withdrawn in 1976 and sold to a small Bradford operator, and was restored during the winter of 1987/8; it is part of the Sheffield Bus Museum collection.

Right:
Maudslay was one of the earliest bus builders, starting in 1905, and in 1948 became part of ACV, with AEC and Crossley. The Marathon III was built between 1947 and 1950, using the AEC 7.7-litre engine, and No 136 was supplied in 1949 to David MacBrayne at Inverness with a 35-seat Park Royal coach body. It was withdrawn in 1966. *Thanks to Derek Hunter*

Above:
Edinburgh Corporation stuck to a glass fibre version of the 1953-style Midland Red front for its later Titans, like No 833, a 1966 PD3A/2 with 70-seat Alexander forward-entrance body. It was withdrawn in 1978.
Thanks to Jim Mason of the Edinburgh Transport Group

Right:
The very last front-engined Leyland Titan was delivered in 1969 to Ramsbottom UDC, No 11 with forward-entrance East Lancs 73-seat body. The Ramsbottom undertaking passed into the new Selnec PTE in 1969. Like other late customers for the Titan, Ramsbottom stuck with the exposed radiator variant in preference to the 'new-look' front version.
Thanks to Dennis Talbot and Mark Prescott of Manchester Museum of Transport

Above:
Sunbeam built trolleybuses from 1931 until 1966. During the World War 2 years Sunbeam built the utility W4 model, and this version with Weymann utility 56-seat body was new in 1944 to Derby Corporation, No 172. There are regrettably very few utility motorbuses or trolleybuses preserved, so vehicles like this are extremely valuable. This offside elevation clearly shows the stark lines of the utility body specification. *Thanks to Mike Dare*

Right:
This Wolverhampton Corporation 1946 Sunbeam W was rebodied by Roe in 1959 with this 60-seat body. No 433 is seen at the Black Country Museum near Dudley alongside the Victoria Square clock which once stood at the top of Railway Drive, Wolverhampton.
Thanks to Keith Bodley and members of the Black Country Museum Transport Group

Left:
A late delivery for the Huddersfield Corporation
trolleybus fleet, a 1959 Sunbeam S7A with 72-seat East
Lancs bodywork. It was withdrawn in 1968 when the
Huddersfield trolleybus system closed and is now
owned by the British Trolleybus Society.
Thanks to David Shepherd

Right:
The last batch of new trolleybuses built for service in
the UK were Sunbeam MF2Bs for Bournemouth
Corporation. These carried stylish Weymann 65-seat
two-door bodies and operated only until the
Bournemouth system closed in 1969. Preserved No 297
is seen at the Black Country Museum.
Thanks to the Black Country Museum Transport Group

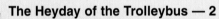
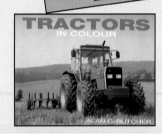